AW, WITH WORDS

Young Writers' 16th Annual Poetry Competition

It is feeling and force of imagination that make us eloquent.

How can I not dream while writing? The blank page gives a right to dream.

South Wigston High School

Edited by Allison Jones

 Young**Writers**

First published in Great Britain in 2007 by:
Young Writers
Remus House
Coltsfoot Drive
Peterborough
PE2 9JX
Telephone: 01733 890066
Website: www.youngwriters.co.uk

SB ISBN 978-1 84431 190 3

Foreword

This year, the Young Writers' *Away With Words* competition proudly presents a showcase of the best poetic talent selected from thousands of up-and-coming writers nationwide.

Young Writers was established in 1991 to promote the reading and writing of poetry within schools and to the young of today. Our books nurture and inspire confidence in the ability of young writers and provide a snapshot of poems written in schools and at home by budding poets of the future.

The thought, effort, imagination and hard work put into each poem impressed us all and the task of selecting poems was a difficult but nevertheless enjoyable experience.

We hope you are as pleased as we are with the final selection and that you and your family continue to be entertained with *Away With Words South Wigston High School* for many years to come.

Contents

George Hart (11)	40
Emma Thompson (12)	41
Nathan Morris (12)	42
Jordan Birtles (11)	43
Cara-Leigh Macfarlane (11)	44
Georgia Garbett (14)	45
Jodie Crewe (13)	46
Ryan Hanney (12)	47
Nicole Blockley (12)	48
Sophie Price (12)	49
Lauren Thomas (12)	50
Jack Morris (12)	51
Abbeygale Follows (12)	52
Imogen Perkins (12)	53
Nathan Francis (12)	54
Ryan Love (11)	55
James Buxton (11)	56
Samuel Latham (13)	57
Leah Hawksley (13)	58
Rachael Johnson (14)	59
Aimee Grocock (13)	60
Shane Rivera (14)	61
Callum Earls (13)	62
James Biddles (14)	63
Ben Vegh (14)	64
Brandon Vaughan (12)	65
Jake Bingham (13)	66
Stefan Smith (12)	67
William Matlock (12)	68
Callum Love (11)	69
Kasey Pugh (12)	70
Laura Mason (14)	71
Arron Grayston (13)	72
Samantha Gaskin (13)	73
Melissa Hawksley (14)	74
Lewis Hurst (13)	75
Emma Gilliver (13)	76
Laura Green (13)	77
Sophie Sawbridge (13)	78
Jade Lyons (12)	79
Adam Langeveld (12)	80
Rushabh Pattani (11)	81

Holly Leftley (13)	82
Ryan Vincent (14)	83
Adam Jamal (11)	84
Emily Machin (11)	85
Jake Tongue (11)	86
Hannah Pigott (11)	87
Ellie Podgers (11)	88
Jack Miller (11)	89
Jade Berry (11)	90
Anikah Malik (11)	91
Joe Ardley (11)	92
James Swingler (12)	93
Alex Pearson (12)	94
Hollie O'Brien (11)	95
Jack Robinson (11)	96
Amber Moscaroli (12)	97
Conor Wilde (11)	98
Olivia Towers (13)	99
Grace Richmond (12)	100
Daniel Towers (11)	101
Lauren Ball (11)	102
Ellie Sheppard (11)	103
Natalie Allen (11)	104
Larissa James (11)	105
Liam Taylor (11)	106
Mylan Charles (11)	107
Kyle Wickwar (11)	108
Anna Snedden (11)	109
Isabel Eaton (11)	110
Lauren Anderson (11)	111
Cariss Warren (11)	112
Lydia Rushton (11)	113
Joseph Storton (11)	114
Leah Allison (11)	115
Brogan Manley (11)	116
Breje Amar (11)	117
Callum Ingall (12)	118
Georgina Carvey (11)	119
Fleur Kingsley-Mills (11)	120
Olivia Hill (13)	121
Eleanor Ainsworth (12)	122
Mason Brown (12)	123

Ryan Westley (11)	124
Kieran White (11)	125
Jamie Hawksley (11)	126
Emily Barnes (12)	127
Jordain Smith (13)	128
Kate Tebbutt (13)	129
Chloe Morris (12)	130
Zain Garratt (12)	131
Grace Neal (12)	132
Ellie Pratt (12)	133
Lucy Henshaw (12)	134
Jordan Elms (13)	135
Ellie McMahon (11)	136
Jordan Tierney (13)	137
Lewis Crane (13)	138
Kiam Read (11)	139
Lucy Cyhanchuk (11)	140
Kelly Wells (11)	141
Alex Vann (12)	142
Rebecca Upsall (12)	143
Leah Macfarlane (14)	144
Harry Hummel (13)	145
Paige Smith (14)	146
Leah James (14)	147
Michael Webster (14)	148
Rebecca Wakeling (13)	149
Samantha Stuart (13)	150
Daniel Probert (13)	151
Ryan Humphreys (13)	152
Chloe Whittle (14)	153
Michelle Small (14)	154
Tom Rowe (13)	155
Rosie Kirk (14)	156
Scott Eaton (14)	157
Nicole Manship (14)	158
Tom Prickett (14)	159
Jessica Dempsey (13)	160
Anthony Stott (14)	161
Megan Heggs (12)	162
Heather Garrigan (13)	163
Jason Green (14)	164
Remi Smith (13)	165

Laura Pugh (13)	166
Beth Corby (11)	167
Kane Bradshaw (11)	168
Rosie-Ann Higgins (11)	169
Jadine Walbrook (12)	170
Reece Johnson (13)	171
Callum Bingham (13)	172
Jake Brimley (13)	173
Ryan Green (12)	174
Harry Demetriou (11)	175
Katie Walker (12)	176
Alex O'Connell (12)	177
Liam Davy (11)	178
Megan Footman (11)	179
Declan Lonergan (13)	180
Sarah-Jane Hammonds (14)	181
Alex Busby (14)	182
Adam Kindleyside (13)	183
Jake Moore (14)	184
Lauren Shepherd (14)	185
Bryony Garrigan (13)	186
Christopher Weston (13)	187
Jacob Smith (12)	188
Lola Witherington (13)	189
Shannen Clark (12)	190
Mark Jones (12)	191
Samantha Higgs (12)	192
Jessica Russell (13)	193
Owen Williams (13)	194
Adam Harlow (13)	195
Jamie Mullineaux (13)	196
Katherine Ardley (13)	197
Max Anderson (13)	198
Ben Cluskey (12)	199
Emma Tones (13)	200
Zara Cook (12)	201
Abi Goyns (13)	202
Robyn Braker (12)	203

The Poems

Disabled For Life

I wonder how it feels to be disabled?
People might look at you, even laugh at you
And make fun about you.
If I was disabled I would try my best to be normal
Disabled people may get sad
But if I was disabled, I would be proud like a lion
When I see people looking at disabled people
I feel like saying, 'Haven't you ever seen a disabled person before?'
Disabled people must feel very angry when that happens
I wonder how it feels to be disabled?

Mehdi Mednini (13)

Rugby

When you look at me
It seems you are calculating my every move
Then I charge and hit with force
And drive forward trying to weaken you
He is starting to hurt
I do not care as long as I get to that line
Then I stumble and hurt my leg
So then I pray that I don't get crushed
This game is brutal but I keep going
So fasten your seat belt here I come
Bang! Crash! I hear
Wondering if I've broken anything
Then I get the ball
And jump fiercely through the air
The next thing I hear is the word, 'Try!'

Samuel Mason (12)

An Abandoned Dog

Being caned every time I barked
Never seeing, just listening
Locked up in a confined space.

Getting thrown on to the street
Not knowing where I am
Seeing bright lights
Being picked up and put into a van.

Put in a big dog kennel
People looking at you all the time
Seeing lots of other dogs being brought in.

Two weeks later being picked up
Put into another car
Being taken to a brand new home
Playing with little children
Going to the park
And always being happy for the rest of my life.

Charlotte Hallam (12)

Brothers And Sisters

Brothers and sisters
Brothers are cheerful
Sisters are annoying
I will tell you why
They make you angry
Brothers are funny sometimes
Sisters make you angry.

Brothers and sisters
Brothers always play with you
Sisters normally make you sad
Lonely is like nothing to do
Something they do makes you cry
Sometimes they disappear and go
So all happy things soon disappear.

Brothers and sisters
Brothers are like best friends
Sisters are like so loveable
They are both so big-headed
Sometimes they are a pain in the neck
They are mean and arrogant
We don't always get on
But I wouldn't want to be without them.

Richard Owens (13)

Children In Baghdad

Bombings all day
Children never seeing the sun
No toys
And no friends to play with
Happiness
Will never be seen in the faces of children
In Baghdad!
Frightened
To take one step out the door
Not knowing
Whether they will get injured or killed
Alone
No one to go to
Tearful
Eyes filled with sadness
And frowning
Because smiling is out of bounds
Cold
And alone
No one to be happy with
Betrayed
Because their family left them behind
Upset
No one to love them
Shaken
Seeing the bloodstains on the door
Wishing they were deaf
So that they would not have to listen to the gunshots
Would you like to be a child in Baghdad?
I thought not.

Kirstey Davis (13)

Homeless Person

Lonely all the time
Will never be happy
Always sad
Always on the streets
Nowhere to go
Upset
Scared all the time
Have family
Never see them
No friends
No one to play with
Or talk to
Tearful
Always thinking - can I go home?
Where is my home?
Eyes full with sadness
Always frowning
Got nothing to smile for
Cold
No family to be happy with
No food
Don't want to go to the shops
Might get injured
Killed
Family, left them
No one to love them
Sometimes wish for death
Because nothing to live for
Would you like to be with your family?
I thought so.

Laura Best (13)

Cancer - Why?

Cancer kills
Cancer is death
Cancer is like an invading army
Cancer is like a bear feeding off your body
Cancer is . . .

Cancer is fear
Cancer is murder
Cancer is like a mouse in your house
Cancer is a kidnapper
Cancer is . . .

Cancer is life-changing
Cancer is a curse
Cancer is like Darth Vader
Cancer is a force field
Cancer is . . .

Why won't cancer die?

Cancer is disturbing
Cancer is like a bad song
Cancer is like a stalker
Cancer is an invader
Cancer is . . .

Cancer is a predator
Cancer is like an everlasting night
Cancer is a robber
Cancer is a shade of death
Cancer - why?

Why won't cancer die?
Why?
Do you think cancer will die?

Drew Spiers (12)

First Love

You've found him at last
He's the one
Or so you think
He's your world
Your everything
Until that one day he says, 'Goodbye.'
All day long you cry
Like a waterfall
You're sorry
But he's just not
You want him back
He's got a new girl
You can't bear it
He was yours
Not hers
He says he loves her
But you love him
He tells you to move on
But you can't
He's your first love.

Adele Dare (13)

Friends

Me and my friends are like a jigsaw
Piece by piece we come together
When we are at our strongest
Somebody tries to break it
But we stay strong.

When somebody is at their worst
We go and see them
Ask them . . .
If they want to hang around with us?

There are about nine of us
The friendliest person of us all is Beth
She is always, always there for me and all of us.

We never get into trouble
We never leave people out.

If somebody is nasty to one of us
We all sort it out!

So look at the jigsaw now
And it will keep growing!

Aimee Masters (12)

A Glue Stick's Life

I sit here on my own
Days on end
Someone takes my hat off and uses me
It is painful
They are using and abusing me
Cutting me up and throwing me about
How would they like it?

Half of my life is up
It is getting worse
From the dreadful pain
From people using me for fun.

My life has been fairly good
From helping all these people
Putting their mistakes together
Or even helping with work.

My life has nearly gone
All I want to say is
Sorry for the sticky situations
I have caused

Cassien Jackman (14)

I Can't Cope Anymore

I can't see a thing
My eyes really sting
It's not just soap
And I can't cope!

People laugh and stare
As though I'm not there
Although I can't see
I can hear . . . trust me.

I just don't understand
I need a helping hand
I am in so much pain
I am going insane.

Life is so hard
Who dealt me this card?
To open my eyes and see
Would be a dream come true for me.

What have I done?
Should I hide and run?
It's a real bore
And I can't cope anymore . . .

Paige Wyatt (13)

What Is The Meaning Of Life?

What is the meaning of life?
What are we here for?
Will we be struck down by a scythe
Or will we live for evermore?

Are we here on purpose
Or even a mistake?
Why were we put on this surface
Of existence that is like a cake?

Are we here to make money
To fulfil our greed?
Or to make it sunny
Sunny for our future breed?

Nial Rees (13)

Turn Back Time

I wish I didn't shout like that
I wish I'd met my grandma
I wish I'd known I'm too fat
Or maybe I've gone too far.

If only I could turn back time
These things I'd love to have done
My family mean more than a dime
So why did I shout at my mum?

My grandad is a funny bloke
And always known as Bill
He would talk and talk to any folk
But at the moment is very ill.

My grandma I would love to have met
As I guess she'd be quite fun
On the motorbike she'd won in a bet
But couldn't afford to run.

I wish I'd known my dog was dying
Of cancer that she had
Then I wouldn't have to sit here crying
And missing her really bad.

Hayley Forbes (14)

Baby Poem

Who am I?
What am I?
Where am I?
What am I doing here?

It is very cold
I feel confused
My head hurts
My stomach aches!

Why can't I see?
What are all these lights?
What is this pain?
Why am I small?

Feels like a thousand knives stabbing me
A ringing inside my head
It is not stopping
I feel strange!

Why can I not breathe?
What is this grumble in my stomach?
Who is this person?
Is she going to get me?
Help me!

Matteo James (14)

Football

I am a football, I sometimes hit the post
I am a football, they always come close
When they hit the ball, I can go in the net
When they kick the ball, I can become wet.

When players hit the ball they often miss
When I get passed I hear the hiss
When I score a goal the players want more
All I can hear is the fans' roar.

And finally when I get in the ground
I always look around.

Jordan Ingram (12)

Poem About School

This is a poem about my school
We go every day because it's the rule
The morning bell rings and the day begins.

We work very hard all morning
Sometimes we find it quite boring
Breaktime's not far away and then we know it's time to play
But then back in class doing science, English, maths.

Then dinnertime is here, the last few lessons are near
Not long now till the end of the day
We all go home and out to play.

Curtis Varnam (12)

Animals

I have a dog
Her name is Mog
Then there's my frog
His name is Splog
All of my pets are different.

Then there's my pig
She is so big
Her name is Stig
She loves to play tig
All of my pets are different.

Then there's my sheep
His name is Treat
He really likes to play hide-and-seek
He has real cheek
All of my pets are different
But they are all very cute.

Hannah Utting (13)

A Time To Think

I've been kicked and hit
I've seen lots of people
Most of them have been hurting me
I'm sore and hurt.

Just leave me alone
Oh no, here comes Ronaldinho
My head's so sore
My body starting to peel away.

I'm feeling down
No one ever notices me for who I am
All people see me for is to play football.

After a game I'm put in a bag with other balls
When it's the start of a match I'm brought out
I'm sitting at the bay.

I'm black and white
Some day I'll be old and wait to be killed
My life will then be over
I will be at rest at last.

Charlie Mee (12)

Hard Life

Every day I get up and ready for school
Trying hard to achieve my ambition
It's hard, I struggle
It's going to take time
It's going to take patience
I want to have a Nissan Skyline
It's expensive, but that's really my ambition
And guess what, I will give all I have got.

Nathan Jefford (13)

Wild And Free

The New Forest ponies run wild and free
They gallop across heathland with thundering hooves
They graze peacefully on hillsides
They dance with graceful movements through the forest
They stand brave and powerful along roadsides.

The New Forest ponies run wild and free
They have long, flowing, golden manes and sun-bleached tails
They have warm sparkling eyes and a calm nature
When you see a herd of New Forest ponies
There is a sparkle of golden colours: browns, bays and chestnuts.

The New Forest ponies run wild and free
They've been on this land for hundreds of years
They trot through villages, proud and brave
They are not frightened, just wary
They come to see the people but stand their distance.

The New Forest ponies run wild and free
They come to see the tourists at the watering holes
With cheeky faces expecting treats
They stand calm and patient, posing for photographs
Their coats are sleek and beautiful
They decide when it's time to leave and disappear back into the forest.

The New Forest ponies run wild and free
They walk slowly along paths
They trot proudly through villages
They canter gracefully through forests
And gallop powerfully over hills.

The New Forest ponies run wild and free
This is how they always should be.

Rosie Trott (12)

Why Are Teenagers So Grumpy?

Why are teenagers so grumpy
Like a cat swishing its tail in anger
Or like a dog growling at the postman?
If only they could smile a bit more
I'm sure they would be more cheerful.

Why are teenagers always sleeping
Like a baby with nothing else to do
Or someone with the flu?
If only they could be more energetic
I'm sure they would be more exciting.

Or ranting or raving
Like someone in a road rage
Or a bear in a bad mood?
If only they could calm down a bit
I'm sure they'd get more done.

Or frowning and not saying anything
As if they've got so much to think about?
They've got no time to talk
If only they would tell people
They'd have less to worry about.

Why are they so bossy and selfish?
Always telling you what to do
And always wanting their own way
Perhaps they should think of other people
Then they might do more giving and less taking.

I'm only 12 so I don't know what it's like
But not for long
When I'm 13 I wonder what I'll be like.

Ellis Arrindell (12)

A Clock

I sit on the wall day after day
Watching the world go round
If you stop and listen
I only make one boring sound.

It's painful when they change my time
They almost break my back
But there's something worse than that
If I stop ticking they just give me a whack!

When my days have ended
And my batteries gone flat
They just put in some new ones
And that's the end of that.

Josh White (11)

What Is The Meaning Of Life?

To meet a film star?
To be sporty?
To drive a fast car?
To live past forty?

To give my love?
To show my hate?
To jump from a plane that flies above?
To never ever forget my mates?

To eat a supersized McDonald's Mac?
To go to Hong Kong?
To not get the sack?
To make up a song?

Georgina Tayler (12)

Hit Me Baby One More Time!

. . . It's now or never, I gotta do this
Forever it was tearing me apart
Then I knew, he was not the one for me
By text I did it, he's over and done
Yep, I'm . . .
Hey!
But!
Oops!
It's then I dropped my baby
Well, nearly
It's kind of tough being me
Well life's not rough here in LA
Hollywood's great
My dream, my passion
Everything you'd want
K-Fed's over
My career's dumped
I'm wearing a stupid blonde wig
To cover my baldness
I'm torn
I'm broken
But my life ain't no toxic waste
But hey, I can beat the rest after all
I am Britney
Britney Spears
Can I put the pieces back together?

Dane Pemberton (12)

A Time To Think

I've been lying here all day long
With no one to see
The crowd soon will be singing along
But I don't know about me.

I'll be kicked around then you'll see
When I'm on the pitch
They will be saying that should be me
And then one falls in a ditch.

The referee gives a red card
When they say, 'It's not a foul!'
I wanted to punch the post hard
When the kick wasn't allowed.

And now I'm still sat here
On my black and white patches
Checking that it was clear
So I can run away for no more matches.

Karl King (12)

The Little Girl

I'm sitting in my room
Don't dare to go down
I can hear her deep breathing at my door
What does she want?
I don't want this night to be the same as last night
She hit me last night, two cuts
She stabbed her fingernails into my arm.

Where's my daddy?
I wonder why he isn't here
I know he doesn't see my mummy hit me
He told me to be strong and fight back
But I know I will still lose . . .
She makes her way into my room
I close my eyes and tell myself
It will be over soon.

Lindsay Storer (13)

The Baby Poem

I am sitting here alone
In this strange place
And it's horrible, I can hardly move a bone
I've tried kicking as best as I can
But that has never worked.
Oh look, I see a light and a very weird man
The light is getting brighter as I move on
Faster and faster, down I go
I can hear someone shouting, 'John, John!'
I feel a slight chill
But not for long
As a towel wraps around me with a frill
I really don't like this
And I start to cry
Being with these people is not bliss!

Heather Brooker (12)

Football

I love football, I play it every day
I play it at school and at home
My life revolves around football
I have loved it since I was young
My dad taught me how to play - he is really good.

Football is so passionate, when you score a goal
When you hit a good ball you know it's going in!
The feeling you get when you score - it's like no other
You feel like the hero of the match!

I feel so tried when I get on the pitch
Because I have worked so hard
The hard work pays off when your team wins
Because you and your team feel so proud.

Then . . . you sit down and have a relaxing afternoon!

Ashley Goodacre (13)

Blind Man

I live in fear
No one cares for me
People plan to mug me while I stand here
Life is sad, sad misery.

But, what is this?
I hear a wonderful sound
With fur as soft as silk
It is my faithful hound
Life is no longer a sad, sad misery
It is far, far less.

Life is no longer a fear
It is no longer a bore
Now that my faithful hound is here
I'm not afraid to go out of the door.

Sam Bennett (11)

Ball

I'm not very happy being a ball
It's not because I'm too big or small
It's because I have lots of shame
When they play a football game
I get all muddy on the field
I really wish to have a bronze shield
I hate it when they leave me to dry
Underneath the sunny sky
The mud dries really quick
Someone please hand me a stick
So I can poke off all the mud
Or leave me in a bath with a sud
Then I roll into the shed
To lie on my comfy bed
Then I'll go gently to sleep
Whilst I do so I'll be counting sheep.

Chloe Smith (11)

I'm Homeless

I haven't seen my family for two whole years
I haven't even got a house
I'm sitting on a cardboard box
Wait, what was that? A cat? A mouse?
I'm really hungry, I want to go in the cafe
Cheese on toast is £2, are they having a laugh?

I am really cold and very sad
I shouldn't have run away from my family
I really miss my mum and dad.

It is starting to get dark
There is nowhere for me to stay
So I lay down near the dustbin
Then it starts to rattle away . . .

James Dunlop (11)

I'm A Library Book

Sitting on a wooden shelf
Next to all my best friends
Waiting for the bell to go
Hear children running up the stairs
Children barging through the door
Children looking at the shelves
They are running up to me
Hands reaching out for me
Taking me to the counter
Getting stamped - it really hurts
Being put in her bag
She is running out the door
And going down the stairs.

Cameron Smith (11)

Maths Is Great, English Too

M aths is great
A nd is my favourite subject
T he time is nearly half-past twelve
H ead for maths when dinner's finished
S ir will be ready to teach

I 'm going to do my homework
S orry, can't come round your house tonight

G reat, I can't wait for tomorrow's lesson
R ight, I'll be here first
E ating my lunch
A ddition and
T imes are the best

E nglish rules
N ever miss my lesson
G reat, it's poetry today
L ate, oh no
I 'm here early to start my day, phew
S ome of my friends are already here
H ate going out my lessons

T oday I won't miss a thing
O h dear, I've forgotten my pencil case
O h no, it's got my English pen in it!

Michelle Orr (11)

I'm A Football

I wait there for someone to kick me
Lonely, only just my friend the bicycle
Hurting I waited and dreading that the bicycle was right
Deep down I felt hurt.
Awaked by the noise of the garage door opening
This was my chance
Someone grabbed me by the head
Ow! I shouted loudly
What is this black hole? It smells vile
There I was waiting
Was I in a black bin?
And there I was in the depth of it
Buried alive in filth and litter.

Callum Taylor (11)

Best Friends

B est friends for life
E nding days we don't want
S tarting now, we won't break
T ime will go quick together

F orever, forever, we're best friends forever
R unning to each other
I love it when I see her
E njoy every minute together
N ever get to end
D ays at school shine
S ee each other on weekdays!

Nancy Cox (11)

I Am A Pen

In the case I sit all day until the zip opens
Another end to the day but I'll be used again
My owner doesn't use me anymore
I am left all the way at the bottom of the case.

Pens always get used again but me, no
Engaged I am to Sir Rubber
No, I am being used for ticks.

Onto the page my tears go
Not me, not a marking pen.

Please don't use me, I need to get married
Love is what I feel for Sir Rubber
Everyone at my party
And orange I will drink
So come on, put me back
Everyone come to the party.

Annabelle King (11)

I'm A Baby

All of a sudden I burst into a world of light
I am so tiny and there are a lot of big people surrounding me
There is a load of people staring at me
I have been trapped in a dark cave for ages
All I can hear is me crying
People are getting jealous because they can't suck their toes
I want to feel safe and secure
They had to take me away so I want my mum
I have been alone for a long time
The people are talking total rubbish
I can't understand what everyone is doing and saying.

Eliza Toorbuth (11)

Sweets

I'm a sticky gooey sweet
Sitting melting, oozing sweetly,
'Pick me up, I'm good to eat!'

In your mouth I'm melting
Oh, that gorgeous taste
Holding that treasure tightly.

Whoosh, whee, whizz, I'm zipped away
Flowing fastly down a tube
The day I'll never forget, *today!*

I've sat in a jar at the sweet shop
Sitting there for donkey's years
Watching sweets being taken
Listening for my name to echo in my ears.

The day I heard my name
Excitement ran through my veins!

Zoë Watts (11)

A Friend

A friend is someone you can trust
A friend would never cheat or lie
A friend is always there for you
A friend would never make you cry.

A friend is helpful, kind and true
A friend would never let you down
A friend comforts when you're sad and blue
A friend would never make you frown.

A friend is like your favourite toy
A friend is with you when you're glum
A friend is a friend, whether girl or boy
A friend is your best chum!

Alexander Mickowski (11)

I'm A Football Boot

I am a football boot who loves going out
Then I go on the pitch where everybody is cheering
The lights turn on
I kick the ball and the game begins.

I pass the ball high and low, hard and soft
The ball goes in our box, get it out, quick
Now we have got a free kick, I curl it and it is in!
We are level now, it is a penalty to win the game . . .
Goal! . . . I love it when I score
1, 2, 3, 4, I have scored so many before
5, 6, 7, 8, when we win it is so great.

Overhead, on the volley, close and take a break
When I am injured I get fit again
The ref blows and we have won
Now to celebrate and have some fun
Come on friends, let's celebrate.

George Hart (11)

Colour

I like red because it's Rosie
I like red because it's for blood
Red is for Man United, the best team.

I like blue
Blue is for Leicester
Blue is for the lovely sky.

Orange is for oranges
Orange is for the sun
Orange is for a crown.

Yellow is for Yellow Pages.

Emma Thompson (12)

Green

My gumshield's green, it's really great
I put it in my mouth to protect my face
I'm writing with my green pen, it's really cool
Cos I've got to do my homework for school
The Hulk is green when he gets mad
He kicks the baddies really bad
Green means go at the traffic lights
Cross with care or you'll die
Trees give us air so we can breathe
Just like our grass is green
Green is the colour of the green-eyed monster
He lives inside us all and sometimes make us look like a fool
The last thing I can think of is a green stem
And that's the end of my big green poem.

Nathan Morris (12)

Blue

Blue is the colour of the sea
Spread out across the world for all to see
Blue is the sky, way up high
Blue is the colour of the ocean
The waves move in a motion
Blue is the colour of a lizard
That walks around in a desert blizzard.

Jordan Birtles (11)

Pink

My favourite colour is pink
I like it because it's bright, also very light
So what do you think?

My favourite colour is pink
I have it in my room
Every time I see it, my mind goes boom
So what do you think?

My favourite colour is pink
I loved pink at first sight
I'd love a big bright kite
So what do you think?

My favourite colour is pink
If I had a price to pay
Pink would make my day
So what do you think?

Cara-Leigh Macfarlane (11)

Why Aren't You Being Yourself?

Why don't you act yourself?
Do you do it to impress others?
Is it for popularity?
Have you got a fear of being different?
Who are you when you're on your own?
Are you aware that with some new friends you might be a nicer person
Or are you happy the way you are?
You try too hard to be someone else
Someone you think is cool or funny
But along the way you lose yourself
You are being manipulated and intimidated.

Georgia Garbett (14)

Me And My Rabbit

As my birthday grew near
I wanted a rabbit more
I was determined to get one
I got everything but a rabbit.

I waited another long year
I was more determined than ever before
Awaiting that wonderful morning
It felt like Christmas
It wouldn't come in a hurry.

One magical morning
I received a baby rabbit
The time we spent together was magical
But on one tragic May morning
My rabbit was no more
Me and my rabbit, together forever.

Jodie Crewe (13)

Why Were We Born?

Were we born to make a difference?
Were we born to have a loving family?
Were we born to go to school and have a good career?
Were we born to have caring and loving friends?
Were we born to help the unfortunate?
Were we born to be a pop star or a footballer?
Were we born to be a doctor or a nurse?

Or were we born to be ignorant and selfish?
Maybe we were born to smoke and be a druggy
Maybe we were born to be a murderer and a thief
And end up in jail for the rest of our life!
Maybe we were born to not care about anyone but ourselves?
Maybe we were born to bully other people
All these questions and one answer
Be yourself and no one else
Try and do the right thing!

Ryan Hanney (12)

A Friend

A friend is . . .
Someone who is always there through thick and thin
Someone who is only a phone call away
A friend is . . .
Someone you can rely on,
Someone who is there to share your thoughts with
Someone to listen, no matter what the subject.

A friend is . . .
Someone you can trust,
Someone who will keep your deepest secrets.
Someone who will never let you down.

A friend is . . .
Someone who supports you
Someone to laugh and cry with
Someone to lean on through both good and bad
A friend . . . is until the end.

Nicole Blockley (12)

My Grandma

A happy, smiling, little woman
Her wrinkly skin
Her sparkling eyes
Which sparkled every time she smiled
A loving and caring mum and grandma
Who made you feel warm and welcome
Her curly, fluffy, white hair
Felt soft and smooth.

When she held me
I felt warm and cosy
The smell of her perfume
Smelt like roses
Sweet
Gorgeous and fresh.

Her house was always clean and spotless
Whenever she knew people were coming round
She would always get sweets, crisps and chocolate bars in.

So when you went round
You'd have something to nibble at
And never be hungry
My grandma!

Sophie Price (12)

My Colour Poem

My favourite colour is pink
When I say pink I wink
When I don't see pink, I sink
Pink is the colour of Piglet
My favourite clothes are pink
My room is pink, my walls are pink
And even my sink is pink
Even my computer is pink
My mouse is pink
If I could I would have my hair pink too
Pink has got to be the world's best colour!

Lauren Thomas (12)

Black, Blue, Green, Red

Blue is for the very important organiser
Blue is a band but they split up
Blue is for the nice warm sea
Blue is for the great big sky.

Green is for the green grass
Green is for the green leaves
Green is for the green bags
Green is for the fat green pepper.

Red is for the sun
Red is for the red rose
Red is for the big juicy tomato
Red is for the red pepper.

Black is boring for the world
Black is for evil
Black is for darkness
Black is for someone's hair colour.

Jack Morris (12)

Pie

I like pie
I don't know why
I really like pie.

I like the pastry
Because it is so tasty
I really like pie.

Steak and kidney
Chicken and mushroom
I really like pie.

Apple and raisin
Pear and peach
I really like pie.

Hot or cold
Custard or cream
I really like pie.

With chips and gravy
Or Smash and peas
I really like pie.

I dream of pie
I talk about pie
I really like pie!

Abbeygale Follows (12)

Food

Food, food, food
It is what gets inside you and me
We put it in our mouths and chew, chew
But food wants to take a bite out of you.

The burgers, the chips and the hot dogs too
They all wanna take a bite out of you
Chips and mushy peas
Don't put them on my plate, please
Sandwiches, a bar and an apple for lunch
They're gonna take a bite and munch, munch.

Food, food, food
It is what goes inside you and me
We put it in our mouths and chew, chew
But food wants to take a bite out of you.

Imogen Perkins (12)

Blue

Blue, the colour of the sea
Which we all can see
Blue is the colour of the sky
Which is way up high
Blue is the colour of my best friend's shoes
Blue, the colour of my nana's eyes
Blue, the colour of the waves
Which crash towards the caves
Blue, the colour of my favourite canoe
Which my brother always knew
Blue, the colour of my garden spade
Which was specially made
Blue, the colour of my pen
Which was discovered by a group of men
Blue, the colour of those sweet
Which are my favourite treats
Blue, the colour of my sister's ball
Which she hits against the wall.

Nathan Francis (12)

Blue

There once was a boy band called Blue
Who thought they knew what to do
They sang the wrong song
That didn't reach number one.

They then went on to prove them all wrong
And reached number one
With a guy named Elton John.

Ryan fell ill
Which made them split
Band mate Antony went into the jungle
Band mate Duncan had a tumble
Band mate Simon still did rumble on.

And that was the end of Blue
Boo-hoo!

Ryan Love (11)

Colours

Colours are where a rainbow stands
Colours can be sweet like all our nans
Colours can be highlights
Which are very, very bright
Colours can be mostly anything!

A colour is red
Which is an emotion for love
A colour is white
Which are stars in the dark night
A colour is yellow
Which is the sun shining in the sky.

Colours are happy
Colours are sad
Colours can be good
And some can be bad.

James Buxton (11)

Flying To Heaven

I'm dead
I wish I was in bed
I don't know why
But I wish I could say goodbye.

I'm flying
I want to know how I've been dying
I want to see my family
I want to see them, they want to see me.

I'm there
I wish I had no care
The golden gates shining
They are almost blinding.

I'm walking
But they are not talking
Twelve disciples all dressed the same
Walking without care, I wish I had their fame.

I'm in
I have only done one sin
God forgave me
It is Him I would like to be.

I'm sleepy
Heaven is so creepy
I can't get used to it
Unlike Hell, it's not a pit.

I'm crying
Not because I've been dying
Because I miss my family
And I know . . . they miss me.

I woke
All because my brother spoke
I'm trying not to scream
Because it was all a dream.

Samuel Latham (13)

Morning Has Not Yet Come

Morning has come
The sun has not set
In fact it has not even risen . . .
Fog and mist take over the sky
As the ice shimmers and shines upon the land
As the snow settles upon the innocent land
Changing its features
Yet I lay awake, watching the life cycle gradually changing
The birds have not yet sung their peaceful songs
Which usually awaken me, urging me to rise
There's no wind howling at the night
Or swaying tree leaves from left to right
Nor the bees buzzing their way to their busy lives
But me . . . I have awoken before the day has begun.

Leah Hawksley (13)

Longing To Hear The Ocean Waves

When I was small, we had holidays by the sea
My parents and sister and me
We played on the beach and lazed in the sun
Everyone happy and having fun
We jumped in the waves and swam in the sea
Oh what a happy time it was for me.

The ocean waves crashing down
Thunderous noise and foaming crests
Children shouting with joy and glee
With ice creams melting in the summer sun
How could anyone be glum?
Not wanting to leave until the golden sunset.

When I was older with children of my own
We had donkey rides along the water's edge
Sandcastles standing tall and straight
Until the waves brought them crashing down
Like the days of my childhood
We didn't want to go home till the sun went down.

My children have now grown up
And have children of their own
Travelling far to new resorts
Beaches now golden and seas so blue
Snorkelling over reefs with fish so colourful
So different from the days of my past.

Now I am old with hearing no more
Walking across the ancient beach
Longing to hear the ocean waves
To bring back those memories
Of the shouts and laughter
From those happy days of my past.

Rachael Johnson (14)

Poem

When you walk in, my whole day gets better
And even when you're not with me
You're in my thoughts always.

You make my life special
Without you I'm incomplete
Incomplete without a heart.

Now my heart is complete
With the love we share
And grows more beautiful with each passing day.

You are with me always
In a smile, a memory, a feeling
Or a moment we share.

I felt my world change
You hugged me
I heard my heart awaken.

There is a dime in a dozen
Then there is a one in a million
But you, you're a once in a lifetime.

I couldn't live, I couldn't breathe
Without you by my side
Will I ever let you go?

Aimee Grocock (13)

Hostage Dream!

All my dreams in my heart to be found and seen
I don't know where to find them
But soon they'll be with me
I dream of escape
From the chains of this life
Which hold me back from freedom
I don't know where it will lead.

I sit in a darkened cell
Not knowing where I am
My only release is in my dreams
Where I seek to find it
To find a place free from pain
Just take me up above
From this devastation
Just please come and save me
Please, please!

I walk along a lonely path to find my answer
Will it come in an hour or will it come in a minute?
I'm waiting for the final contact
All I want is a bullet
Just cant bear waiting anymore.

I hear footsteps coming towards me
Could it be my mind
Or could it be my destiny?
The cell door opens with a furious push
My head against the floor
Blade against my neck, *slash!*
My life slips away but my soul finds freedom
Dream, dream.

Shane Rivera (14)

Biggest Game Of The Season

On the 20th of March 2007
We were going to football
To watch a big game
Man United vs Barcelona.

We bought our tickets from the office
And then walked in
We sat down like falling snow
To cheer the boys below.

The referee blew his whistle
And began to play the game
It went 1-0 to United
And home fans went wild.

After half-time the teams came out
The crowd began to shout
After five minutes Barcelona then attacked
The Spanish boys equalised.

Eighty-eight minutes Barcelona attack
The ball comes up
Eto'o shot and
Scored the winner.

Callum Earls (13)

Football Moments

Here is my chance
My first training opportunity
It is all happening
All at the same time as well
I step onto the grassy green
My boots glistening next to me
It feels like magic
Like a new feeling
As my first game approaches
Then the nerves kick in
The sun is ready
To see me start my dream
Halfway through now
The way, I don't see how things worked
It's all clear now
The way of life
They both stop and start
Everything changes
Until it turns again
Then in front of me the ball
No one around me
A clear run for glory
The ball crashes into the net
That is it, it's over.

James Biddles (14)

A Broken Arena

The quiet sound of an empty football ground
The sound of the wind blowing
The goal pegs blowing onto the post
It is so quiet here.

The view inside the ground
With sixty thousand empty chairs all folded up
Around the stadium with the blackbirds singing
On the trimmed green grass.

When the sun goes down the birds are flying off
While stood there in the dark emptiness
Of an abandoned football arena
It is now getting scary.

Went on the pitch, sat down on the cold grass
Looking around trying to find a light source
In this tomb of darkness
In the cold air, running towards the goal.

So now climbing up this big white goal frame
Sitting on top of the crossbar
With the gold stars which shine down
Upon the ground.

Ben Vegh (14)

A Time To Think

I love going on holiday, especially on a sunny day
I love to play in the sand and in the sea I stand.

I like to lick the dripping ice cream
It makes me feel like I'm in a dream.

I always go to the theme park
I ride on the roller coasters that are fierce as sharks.
(And they give off sparks.)

I love to go to the swimming pool
Because it's really cool.

On holiday I love to go shopping
When I do I'm never stopping.

I love going on holiday
It's really upsetting when you have to leave
But I know we will come back another day.

Brandon Vaughan (12)

A Time To Think

Why me? Why did you have to pick me?
There are loads of other footballs in there
I'm just a plain, old, boring ball
I've been sat in there for years
Talking to all my mates
It's boring in there
But it hurts when you're getting kicked about
And hitting the net
I just want to be left alone
With my mates
Those great big meanies who picked me
I hate them
But I ask myself, why me?
Just, why me?

Jake Bingham (13)

A Time To Think

I've been kicked too many times
I've got no mates
But I think all the people like me
When they kick me I get a dent in me
But I get back up.

I like it when I get hit
I think it tickles
When I hit this white thing, it hurts
I want to be another one
But I'm padded
Nothing can hurt me.

Please let me go free
I'm bored, keep getting hit
I sometimes hit the net
And everyone gets off their chairs and cheers!

Stefan Smith (12)

I Hate Being A Football

I hate being a ball
I always get kicked around
I'm not very tall
I am so small.

It gives me such a headache
I'm always in such a rush
Just hating it when I'm awake
I always blush and get such a sugar rush!

I wish I was in bed
Why do I have to be a ball?
Can't I be a flower?
As onto the pitch I crawl
I wish I was dead!

William Matlock (12)

In The Trenches Of World War I

Shocked and scared the soldiers who wait
Aren't sure what's going to happen.
All dying and wanting to escape
Fire! They all shoot in pattern.

Unsure of all the events that will take place
They're sick and worried.
A grenade thrown at their face - what a disgrace!
Then all the troops scurry.

Bang! The explosive went
Yes, it just missed.
Because they all dived
All feel blessed.

Then it goes quiet
We get out of the trenches . . .
And play a game of football!

Callum Love (11)

Start Of It All

I stand here alone
In a wet dreary shelter
No company there is
Starving, I could eat a horse
The start of it all
Colder and colder
Throat about to drop out
Clothes are rotten
I need a miracle
I scream out,
'Oh Lord,
You have killed so many people
Stop it now.'
It still goes on
My tummy groans
I see somebody
I say, 'Help me!'
They get help
They get a stretcher
I find energy
To lift myself up
On that stretcher
I have found the miracle!

Kasey Pugh (12)

Friends Forever

A friend is someone you can trust
Someone who you can share secrets with
Friends should be a part of everyone's life
They are always there for you if you ever need them
That is a true friend
True friends are hard to find and lucky to have
Friends understand you when you're in a mood
And try and help you with advice
Friends care, friends share
We need friends everywhere
Friends are one in a million!

Laura Mason (14)

Drugs

Mr Independent
Mr Never-Understud
Oh my God
I shouldn't have done drugs.

Sitting on the park bench all alone
I know I should have said no.

Wasted my life
Taking them
Whatever you do
Don't take them.

I plead with you
Whatever you do
Don't take *drugs!*

Arron Grayston (13)

My Eyes

As night falls, light fades away
And darkness comes quickly
My eyes cannot see now.

The sky turns from blue to black
And yet my eyes see there
The moon and stars are bright and clear
My eyes see far away now.

I close my eyes and go to sleep
And think of all they've seen now
They need rest and so do I
My eyes see only black now.

As daylight comes, they open
And look around to see up now
Darkness gone, colours appear
My eyes see many things now.

Samantha Gaskin (13)

Untitled

There is no one here
I'm all alone
All I have is
My bone.

Life is awful
Out on the streets
With everything
But friendship.

No one to love
No one to love me
Life is lost
Amongst the world.

My bone is all
My memories
All my life.

I see people
Pass and stare
I open my eyes
So I look cute
But all they do is
Shoo me away!

Melissa Hawksley (14)

BMX Track

Waiting at the top
Your nerves everywhere
All my friends flying through the air
And there I am waiting at the top.

I'm ready to go down
Down the quarter pipe
It's my turn to go down, people are waiting
Now I'm going down, I feel like fainting.

Speeding along the course
Doing all the jumps
Going down another ramp
Dodging all the humps.

All these things happening so fast
All these things . . .
I love to move fast
I love the BMX track!

Lewis Hurst (13)

Love Poem

I love you -
For being the one
And for loving me back
I love you -
From the bottom of my heart
I will love you for eternity.

I love you -
For being thoughtful
And caring as can be
I love you
For making me happy
Through the bad times as well.

I love you -
For all these emotions
I love you for being you.
I love you
For being there
This is what love is!

Emma Gilliver (13)

Your Life

It's your day
It's your week
It's your month
It's your year
It's your life.

Live life your way
Be who you are
Never change for anyone
Not even for the one you love
It's your life.

Your life is full of possibilities
Life is full of dreams
Life is full of ups and downs
And isn't always what it seems
It's your life.

You never know where life will take you
You will never know when life will end
Life is a journey, see it to the end
Life is a challenge, meet it
It's your life
It's your life!

Laura Green (13)

Saying Goodbye

After school
One Thursday evening
My mother called me in
Along with my brother
And sat us down
And told us the words
We didn't want to hear.

Behind the hearse
Drowning in sorrow
Going over uneven ground
Thinking of the last time I saw
And spoke to him.

In the church
Sitting in silence
Holding a hanky
For each tear that falls.

He lays there
Lonely and emotionless
With no feelings
And no thoughts.

Listening to what's said
About my grandad
And hearing his favourite tunes
Is all so sad
And so sudden
My grandad was a hero
World War I and II.

He fought his best
And survived until that day
My grandad loved me so
In every single way.

Sophie Sawbridge (13)

Food's The Best

Food is yummy
It gives you that feeling in your tummy
There are foods I dislike
And foods I like
Foods that are spicy and hot
Foods that are tasty and some that are not
Some that are sweet
A real treat
Some that are not yummy
And give me a pain in my tummy
Overall, food is the best
And it beats the rest!

Jade Lyons (12)

The Beauty Of Colour

Blue, blue, the colour of the sea
Clean and pure just for you and me.
Blue, blue, like the clear bright sky
With the hot glowing sun shining in my eye.

Green, green, field after field
What, who knows, will they eventually yield?
Green, green, the leaves on the trees
Some young, some old, but all grown from seeds.

Yellow, yellow, for flowers and spring
The sun and the warmth make you jump and sing.
Yellow, yellow, the fields of wheat
Growing strong and steadily in the heat.

White, white, the clouds so bright
Sailing calmly by at such a height.
White, white, the moon so mysterious
Out at night to shine and guide us.

Red, red for anger and hate
Especially when you're annoyed and late.
Red, red, roaring flames up high
Can burn down a forest in the blink of an eye.

Adam Langeveld (12)

Colours Outside

Red
Is the early morning lightening the sky
With glass glimmering in the buildings so high.

Orange
Are the autumn leaves swaying on the trees.

Yellow
Is the honey made from the stinging bees.

Blue
Is the sky that makes a sign above.

Purple
Is the blanket falling on you and me.

Rushabh Pattani (11)

Child Abuse

In my dark room
Where I sit all day
In the corner awaiting my nightmare
I daren't move as they will know I'm here
I dare not even blink or breathe.

Bang! I hear someone on the stairs
I shiver with fear
I am getting ready for what happens next
I promised myself I wouldn't cry today
But already I can feel the wetness
Running down my cheeks.

The door begins to open
And the light comes beaming in
I wipe away the odd tears
As the dark shadowy appearance
Comes towards me
Before I know it
I am lying there like sharp knives
I am getting hurt everywhere.

I ask myself, why me?
But it is now a daily thing
Although I am only six
I understand what my father does to me
But . . . I don't know some places he goes.

I am but six
My skin is bruised and I don't look the same
I love my mummy and daddy but why don't they love me?

Holly Leftley (13)

Hobo Billy

I've lived out on the streets
Since I was ten
Scrounging money and food off people
I can't even wash
Or clean myself up
Or even eat when I want to.

When a young boy gave me one pound
I decided to enter the lottery
When I listened on my little radio
I heard my numbers called out.

And now I'm looking out of my mansion window
Out on the street I used to live on
And now I've won 10 million pounds
I can get whatever I want.

Ryan Vincent (14)

The Loss Of My Cat

Black as the darkest night
Flexible as a circus team
Faster than the lightning
That strikes across the land.

Fur, black yet shiny
Face, cute yet vicious
These are the things
I think of when I hear her name.

This is a memory
Of the best cat in the world
She was looked up to, adored and blessed
Until that weary day arose
Her name . . . Ice.

She ran with excitement
The world in her paw
Maybe too much excitement
And then it came, suddenly.

Clever, very, very sophisticated
Beauty, came and went with ease
Danger, with its owner came.

A metal, heartless monster of a beast
Came roaring as it polluted the world
It hit with a force
A miaow with her last breath
This was the end of Ice.

Adam Jamal (11)

Colours

Blue
Blue is the colour of the deep blue sea
The waves that crash about so free
The dolphins and the sharks below
Will rise to see the ocean's show
Blue is a delicate, yet fierce colour.

Purple
Purple is the colour of velvet so deep
The colours I see as I drift off to sleep
The yonder horizon I see in my dreams
The colours that float on countryside streams
Purple is a rich and luxurious colour.

Black
Black is the colour of the deathly night
The colour that sees all the witches in flight
The colour that brings death to the land
And makes all men fearful to stay where they stand
Black is a deathly, mysterious colour.

Pink
Pink is the colour of little girls
The colour of the ribbon that ties up their curls
The colour of flowers that wave in the breeze
The colour of the blossom on the cherry trees
Pink is a calm, tranquil colour.

Red
Red is the colour of Valentine's Day
The colour that helps bring love to that day
The colour that looks like blood has been shed
The blood on the battlefield after soldiers have fled
Red is a bright and loud colour.

And finally . . .
Colours, colours, they're everywhere
Red is for anger, deep blue for despair
Green for envy, pink for love
White is the colour of the peaceful dove
Colours help the world go round.

Emily Machin (11)

Blue

My favourite colour is blue
It can be a girl's colour too
Blue is the colour of the sky
And also the colour of my eye
Blue makes me feel calm
Blue makes a night sky
It's also in blueberry pie
I have a blue bed
Much better than red ·
Blue makes me feel cool
Just like a swimming pool
That's my favourite colour blue!

Jake Tongue (11)

Chocolate

I love chocolate
Love the crunchy bite
Milk, minty, dark or white.

I love chocolate
It's what I always buy
Why is it unhealthy?
Why, oh why?

Muffins or cakes
I don't mind
Just give me chocolate
Any kind.

So give me chocolate
Give me more
Cos it's the food
That I adore.

Hannah Pigott (11)

Colours

Colours are everywhere
Every time you look, they're there
Bright colours, pale colours
Dark colours, light colours
Colours that shine like gold
But colours as dull as mould
There are colours like jewels
And colours like tools
Colours make me happy
Colours make me sad
Colours change my mood
From good to bad
Yes, colours are strange
In different ways
I hope you enjoy my poem for days!

Ellie Podgers (11)

Also

I really like chips
They taste good on my lips
I also like beef
I get it from a chief
I also like ice cream
It makes me scream
I also like soup
It's like a loop-the-loop
I don't like pears
They give me the scares
I also don't like mash
It looks like trash
I also . . .

Jack Miller (11)

Colour Pink

Pink, pink, it makes me think
Of all things oh so girly
Bows, ribbons, lips and hearts
Round pigs with tails so curly.

Pink nail polish, lipstick
And sometimes even hair
Some lads think it's not for them
And some lads just don't care.

Pink, pink, boys seem to hate
But us girls really love it
Light and bright and baby too
And sunsets up above it
Pink!

Jade Berry (11)

Red

The poison ran down my throat, burning as it went
I grabbed the razor-sharp knife
I pierced the knife into my heart
It caused me some bloody strife.

Sweltering heat, flames all around
All alone in a cell
Then appeared the horns of the Devil
I had arrived in Hell.

I was in Hell, with hate in the air
I thought with angel's wings I'd fly
But when given devil horns
All I could do was cry . . .

I thought it would be an easy way out
But now that I am dead
I'm all alone, in a world of the Devil
Surrounded by nothing, but red . . .

Anikah Malik (11)

Food

Everybody
Eat some food
If you don't
You ain't a cool dude
Deep-fried lobster
Fresh-baked bread
Or even just
A chicken leg
What you eat
Is up to you
I like apples
How about *you*?

Joe Ardley (11)

Chocolate

C hocolate is something you can't go without
H eavenly, creamy, without a doubt
O ne more chunk, again and again
C hoices are enormous, pick that one
O ut of chocolate just go to the shop
L eave the house but not for pop
A treat that's good for an unborn baby
T ummies rumbling, chocolate maybe
E aten on any day.

What would the world be without chocolate?
I know . . . *boring!*

James Swingler (12)

Hrothgar

Over water, through the waves
Working at the oars like slaves
To Hrothgar
On the hills a watchman sees
A boat that might just be the key
To Hrothgar
They start their journey at Land's End
Over hills and round the bends
To Hrothgar.

In the darkness of the night
Will Grendel come, well he just might
To Hrothgar.

Beowolf can't do any harm
In bringing forward Grendel's arm
To Hrothgar.

Alex Pearson (12)

Colour!

Looking at the orange sky as the sun comes up
Seeing it brighten our lives is a really nice look
As the blue sky comes up
With the fluffy white clouds
But as the rain clams up
Happiness is not around
Darkness comes over our day
All the sky turns dingy grey
As the rain hits the ground
All the grass turns muddy brown
Night-time appears
The twinkling stars gather here.

Hollie O'Brien (11)

Beans

Beans, beans, beans
Butter beans
Baked beans
Big fat lima beans
Runner beans
Those are just a few.

Green beans
Black beans
Kidney beans
Chilli beans
Don't forget magic beans
Jumping beans too.

Pea beans
Pinto beans
Don't forget shelly beans.

I like any kind of beans
Including Jelly Beans.

Jack Robinson (11)

Beowulf

Beowulf is a hero
How people cheer his name
Paying a debt for his father
Wasn't just a game
He beat the sea-hag
And Night Stalker too
Now Heorot Hall
Would be safe for you.

Amber Moscaroli (12)

My Monster

The food he eats is quite amazing
Snails, frogs and all animals you can think of
He eats these on a daily basis
Some say he is quite atrocious
Some say he is an animal
But all I know is that he is disgusting
He eats food all different colours
Such as orange, pink, red, brown
And of the colours of the rainbow
He eats all different shapes too
Squares, rectangles and all other shapes
He is the weirdest you will ever meet
And all I know about him is that he is my monster.

Conor Wilde (11)

Blinded

Blinded for life
Darkness
Loneliness
I walk out the door
People laugh
I wonder what to do
Cry or run
The rest of my life must go on
I feel lost inside
No one to love
No one to see
No one to hold
Just a guide to take with me
My dog.

Olivia Towers (13)

The Warrior

I am the warrior
Brave and proud
Fierce screams are heard all around
I wish I was free

I am the warrior
Important and strong
But in this battle I will not live long
I wish I was free

I am the warrior
People look up to me
For some I'm a hero, others I'm the enemy
I wish I was free

I am the warrior
Forever alone
In my lonely armour as heavy as stone
I wish I was free.

Grace Richmond (12)

Man U

Man U are the best
Any team thinks they're good
But we'll put you to the test
We'll beat you all
We'll keep playing and we'll never fall!

Daniel Towers (11)

A Poem About My Evil Brother

It's not fair that my brother pulls my hair
It's not fair that my brother pulled me off my chair
It's not fair that he grazed my knee
It's not fair that he's mean to me.

It's not fair that he robbed my phone
It's not fair that he lives in my home
It's not fair that he clears our plates
It's not fair that he rings his mates.

It's not fair that I'm stuck with him
Because I'd rather just throw him in the bin!

Lauren Ball (11)

Love Is . . .

Love is holding hands on the beach
Love is when people you love lift you up to reach
Love is when people make you feel good
Love is when you know you could
Love is when people sweep you off your feet
Love is when two people meet
Love is when people stay together forever
Love is when people never say never
That is what love is!

Ellie Sheppard (11)

Love Is . . .

Love is when you stare at the phone for hours waiting for him to call
Love is when you can't sleep because all you can think about
is his smile
Love is when you sit on the computer all day waiting for that stupid
noise to go off
And you can talk to him all day.

Love is when he takes you out on your first date
Love is when all he talks about is football and you listen
Love is when you both take your last breath together
Love is when you have your first and last dance together.

Love is when you hold hands in the rain
Love is when you run to him with tears running down your face
And he still calls you beautiful.
Love can hurt and you stand all day in the rain so no one can see
your falling tears
But love is all around you!

Natalie Allen (11)

If Only . . .

If only all make-up was free
If only money grew on trees!

If only everyone stopped all wars
If only we all helped charities poor!

If only Christmas was every day
If only rain was just in May!

If only boys were banished from the world
If only my brother wasn't such a nerd!

If only my brother didn't pull my hair
If only my brother was always fair!

If only we could drive at 15
If only my mum would stick with nicotine!

If only spiders weren't crawly and big
If only I'd gone to *that* famous live gig!

Larissa James (11)

Liverpool

Liam is my name and football is my game
In my house there are footballs everywhere
My family are all serious Liverpool fans
My mum hates football, so she gets the mardies!

Taylor is my second name
One day you'll see it on a Liverpool shirt
Anfield is the best ground we've ever been to
Yes, we beat Chelsea in the FA Cup
Liverpool are the best team and you know they are!

Liam Taylor (11)

The Reds

We support the Reds
Sometimes in our beds
And Henry said
Never watch us dead.

They have just got a new ground
We watch our team around
We can all hear the sound
Of Henry collecting his pounds!

Mylan Charles (11)

My Mum

My mum helped me every day
She let me go out and play
She would help me through anything
Even the silliest thing.

My mum was very nice
She made me laugh once or twice
I wish she stayed with me forever and ever
Then she wouldn't die, no, never, never.

I loved her so
No matter where she would go.

Kyle Wickwar (11)

Penguin Danger

Diving down through small ice cracks
Snatching fish for dinner
My friends waiting
Hopefully they will not have gone.

I come up out of the water
But where are they?
They wouldn't leave
But then I see it
As white as a sheet, a hungry-looking . . .
Polar bear.

Is this it?
The end of a small penguin's precious life
He runs towards me
I try to run, but no use
I take a few steps and close my eyes . . .
And . . .

. . . I am pulled away by a shadowy penguin-like shape
It pulls me behind an iceberg
Who is it?
It is a friend come to save me!
At last, I am *safe!*
I hope!

Anna Snedden (11)

My Dog Rolo

Floppy ears
Shining eyes
Pointy teeth
And slobber chops
Fluffy head
Rumbling belly
Loves sausage, bacon and chicken
Silky black and tan coat
Loves to walk forever
Chucks himself on the floor
And sleeps for hours
Wakes up happy
Running round
Eating what he can find
Has lots of blankets
Five at least
Likes to snuggle up to them
Very cute all the time
Especially when you have food
Likes to play for ages
And pinches socks and underwear.

Isabel Eaton (11)

Mother

Eyes shimmering like pools of blue
Skin as soft as a baby's bottom
Teeth gleaming in the midnight moon
Smelling as fresh as a dozen roses.

Clothes cute and stylish
She has a marvellous sense of style
When walking to the local shop
She marks her territory
With the fresh scent of her perfume.

Cuddles, warm and cosy
Her voice is like a sweet angel
Her cooking is like she is a professional.

When she helps around the house
She leaves her excellent perfume smell
So that it smells lovely and clean.

When I'm ill
She helps me do things
She does my laundry
Cooks my dinner
My mum is my *hero!*

Lauren Anderson (11)

My Little Sister

My little sister Halle
Eyes like little pearls
Lovely soft hair like silk strings
Her lips so thin and small
Her little laugh in the mornings
I walk in sad
Then I see her
She makes me smile
She is so cute
Her skin is so soft and gentle
She smells like baby shampoo
She was born in September
As sweet as a strawberry
Her cuddles comfort me
And so when she sleeps
I love her so much.

Cariss Warren (11)

Giraffe Disaster

My long spotty neck
Reaches my food
Top of the trees
I get my luscious leaves.

My baby eats my dropped leftovers
She gobbles away
Like a wild cat eating its prey.

But what's that I see?
A burning tree, a spreading fire?
We must leave now, it's spreading fast
Please don't die baby
Not now, not from all that smoke.

Lydia Rushton (11)

Football

Players zooming down the pitch
Dribbling round opponents
Passing the ball from player to player
Different teams in different colours
Battling for the cup.

The penalty spot as white as a star
Waiting for the player to shoot
Blasts the ball through the net
And flies out the stadium.

The crowd cheer
The players hug
While the opponents sigh
The coach runs onto the pitch
The team who scored leap with joy
While the opponents take a kick-off.

Some of the players chase the ball
Whereas some don't
The ball gets kicked off the pitch
Then is back in by a player throwing it.

Control the ball
With head and body
And kick it to a teammate.

The whistle blows
The game has ended
The winning team
Win the cup.

Joseph Storton (11)

The Beard

My friend's dad has a giant frizzy beard
It is black with bits of food stuck in it
It always looks like lots of tarantulas piled up on top of him
And argh, it does give out an awful smell
Has he just been down to the sewers?
Yuck!

Leah Allison (11)

My Rabbit

Beady eyes gleaming in the sunlight
Black
Round
Looking this way and that.

Hair as soft as can be
Different colours
Smudging together
Ginger, white and black
Whiskers tickling my nose
As he climbs up my chest
My rabbit is as cute as can be!

Brogan Manley (11)

The Seaside

The sun rises as it reflects its shadow to the blue sparking sea
As the gentle waves come towards the sand.

Sand is so soft to touch like a cloud
Also it can be fun to play with.

Some little empty shells, sometimes stand on the little desert
While crabs and little creatures come and look for their houses.

Pebbles and seaweed clatter everywhere at the seaside
Where people can see them.

As the sun goes down, everything is quiet and calm
Back where it started from.

Breje Amar (11)

Colours

Colours, colours everywhere on your clothes and in your hair
Lots of browns and lots of blacks
Sometimes found in big green sacks
The sky is full of blues and greys
Mainly blue on summer days
The sun is yellow, the stars are bright
Some cars are silver, but sheep are white
Colours, colours in the air
Oh my gosh, they're everywhere
Colours, colours on the ground
Oh my gosh, they're all around.

Callum Ingall (12)

Beowulf And The Sea-Hag

Strong as an ox
Sly as a fox
The bravest man in Geatland
Long hair flowing
Sharp sword swishing
The most fearless man in Geatland.

Greasy hair hanging
Sharp claws scratching
Rotten teeth grinding
Evil heart pounding
Ugly eyes staring
Massive nostrils flaring
This devil is the sea-hag.

On punch, one kick
One scratch, one bite
One good, one evil
Two enemies unite
One lunge, one swish
One head on the ground
The sea-hag was beaten
No one around
Victorious, victorious.

Georgina Carvey (11)

Popcorn Poem

My best mate loves popcorn
Her favourite flavour is toffee
She has it with her coffee
Everyone calls her Popcorn Polly.

She gulps it down so fast
Morning, evening and night
I don't know how she does it
She gives us all a fright!

At breakfast she likes plain on toast
At lunch with tomato sauce
And at dinner she has toffee with broccoli
With popcorn pie!

Fleur Kingsley-Mills (11)

Turning Back Time

I wish I could turn back time
So people could make it mine
People didn't realise how happy I was
But I had to let that feeling go
Now time goes by so slow
I wish I could go back and change my ways
The little piece of that happiness is still there
But not everyone I know
I don't know why it was so complicated
I suppose I should have waited.

Olivia Hill (13)

My Beowulf Poem

A brave and loyal friend to have
Not loud nor boastful nor rude
A man who is rather quiet
Unless you are a man who can afford to challenge him.

A strong and powerful man
But doesn't make sure others know it
He is a hero, but not for fame or money
But for the feeling and pride that follows.

He is taller than his thanes
And does not boast about it
He would show a good example
To those who think it matters.

This man is a friend for all
You may or may not know this
But this man that I speak of
Goes by the name of . . . Beowulf!

Eleanor Ainsworth (12)

Yum

Pasta slides down your throat
Lots of shapes
Big shapes, small shapes
They are all so tasty, yum . . .

Fruit, fruit is very tasty
Apples, oranges, bananas and pears
Any fruit, I don't care
My favourite of all is a kiwi, yum . . .

Chips are not healthy
They make you fat
I don't care
They are delicious, yum . . .

Mason Brown (12)

My Footy Team

My footy team is Chelsea
My footy team is the best
My footy team has the best players
My footy team beats everyone in the world
My footy team has the best managers
My footy team has the richest chairman
My footy team has my best player
My footy team is the best!

Ryan Westley (11)

Seaside

Pack the car up
Make sure you've got the sandwiches
Lock the front door
Let's get going.

Go along the bumpy roads
Up hills, down hills
The car rattles and shakes
We are here!

The blue clouds
The sparkling sea
The soft sand
The burning hot sun
We have come to the seaside!

Kids running round
Buckets and spades everywhere
People sitting in deckchairs relaxing
People having picnics under the sun
I have come to the seaside!

I build sandcastles
I have a dip in the sea
I go around the arcades and shops
I have an ice cream
I want to go home!

At last night has dawned
I grab a blanket
I get in the car
I go to sleep and dream
My seaside journey has finished!

Kieran White (11)

My Mum's Sunday Dinner

Best Sunday dinner ever
Does whatever I want
Mash, I like it soft and sweet
Smells beautiful
Veg is fantastic
Always lots of food left
And always tastes beautiful
Yorkshire pudding
I like it a little bit soft
Beef smells brilliant, tastes brilliant
Mash, I like it soft and I like it piled up
I don't like boiled potatoes
I don't have gravy, I have red sauce
I think gravy is horrible
Red sauce is the best with Sunday dinners
Especially my mum's Sunday dinner
Sometimes I have corned beef
I don't dip that in red sauce
That would be horrible.

Jamie Hawksley (11)

Black

Black is assumed a dull colour
Although it is not very pretty
I like black T-shirts and jeans
And I especially love my black kitty.

I like to wear my black leather boots
Black suede boots are good too
I express my moods with colours
Black means a neutral mood.

I love black hairbands
They are suitable for school
Black beads and bangles
Black is cool.

Emily Barnes (12)

What Am I?

At night is when I work the best
A cuddle, a squeeze is what I'm for
My owner talks to me more than the rest
I really don't need anything more.

But what is this that I see?
It's cute and snug and ever so soft
I can't believe she's on my territory
I really hope I'm not put in the loft.

I may have lost an ear and an eye
But you shouldn't put me in the bin
I know I'm going, I'm starting to cry
There is the box, I'm going in.

I'm now in the dark in a box
There are socks, books and the core of a pear
I now wish I was a bird or a fox
And not a teddy bear.

Jordain Smith (13)

My Heart

My heart pains
It's so sore
When I saw you lying there on the floor
As I looked down a note's what I found
Written to me
As plain as I could see
As I read it I burst into tears
My make-up started to smudge and smear
My heart keeps askin'
Why did he leave?
Why did he go
When he said he loved me so?
Now in a coffin is where you're for keeps
With you always, in my dreams.

Kate Tebbutt (13)

Speak The Mind Of A Victim

Bullying hurts, here he comes again
Big Buster Ball comes barging in.

My heart bets faster, here it goes
Everyone stares but nobody knows.

I run to the bathroom and lock myself in
I'm not surprised God doesn't forgive his sins.

Louder and louder I hear his footsteps on the floor
I get knocked out for about an hour or more.

Tomorrow it all happens again
Big Buster Ball comes barging in.

Chloe Morris (12)

In My Dreams

If I could be anywhere in my dreams
I would be somewhere weird
But somewhere that suits me
And means a lot to me.

It would be somewhere quiet
Somewhere calm
Somewhere without any fright
But somewhere that means a lot to me.

It could be here
It could be there
It could be in Africa
Or maybe even India.

But the thing you want to know
Is where I would be
Where would I be . . .
In my dreams.

Zain Garratt (12)

You Love Someone

Y ou love someone, who loves someone else
O ne person who changes your life
U nrequited love

L ove hurts
O ne person who you know is the one
V oices tell you to forget
E ven though your heart is saying otherwise

S omeone you love and will love forever
O ne person you will never forget
M aybe you'll get over him?
E ven in your dreams?
O ne time that you are happy is when you were with him
N o one knows how you really feel
E veryone is against you.

Grace Neal (12)

Chavs And The Things They Do!

As the chavs waddle down the street
The geeks get prepared for a beat
Meanwhile little babies are taking a nap
One of the chavs wakes them and shouts, 'Braap!'

As the chavs say, 'Pow!'
The geeks say, 'Ow!'
Meanwhile the babies wail
One of the chavs then stands on a dog's tail.

Those are the things that chavs do
They are the things that make us shout, 'Poo!'
So, geeks get prepared
Because here come the chavs, *beware!*

Ellie Pratt (12)

Wish You Were Here

I wish you were here on the golden sand
I wish you could see the gorgeous sunset
I wish you were here to feel no breeze
I wish you could see what I could see.

I wish you were here to have a cocktail with me
I wish you could see the bright sun shining
I wish you were here to see the calm clear ocean
I wish you could see what I could see.

I wish you were here in the calm warm evening
I wish you could see the night blue sky
I wish you were here to have a dance with me
I wish you could see what I could see.

I wish you were here to sunbathe with me
I wish you could see the beautiful seashells
I wish you were here to have such fun
I wish you could see what I could see.

Lucy Henshaw (12)

Sinon

Yesterday I found a new colour, it's called 'Sinon'
It's the colour when I'm rushing down the hill
It's the colour of the new baby's skin
It's the colour of the newborn puppy
It's the colour when the world comes to an end
It's the colour of the girl who has just been dumped
It's the colour of the crowd when Liverpool has just scored.

Jordan Elms (13)

Autumn Forecast

The lively wind is coming
And the leaves are sailing by
The rain is soaring down to earth
As the trees start to sigh!

The flowers cry bye-bye my seeds
As they run off through the sky
While the lively wind soon dies out
And the winter learns to fly!

Ellie McMahon (11)

The Football

I am an Adidas football
I like being a football
I get looked after well
Sometimes I get stored
Sometimes I get blown up
A man just coming in, he's picked me up
We are in his car now
We've been driving for hours
We are here
Why are there lots of men?
Why is there a whistle?
Ouch! Ouch! Ouch!
Why are they kicking me
Oh no, I am in a match
I'm going to end up like my brothers
Phew, the match is over
Finally I'm going home to be pumped up
I'm home now
Oh yes, he's brought out a sponge
Oh yes, that feels good, oh yes
He will just put me on the rack now
With the other balls
I wish my brothers and sisters were here.

Jordan Tierney (13)

A Time To Think . . .

I hate being a glue stick being rubbed all the time
It's so boring, why couldn't I have been a lollipop?
If I had arms and legs I'd give them a good kickin'
I wish I could just walk down the road and away
But with my kind of condition that's not that easy
Oh no, here she comes again!

Lewis Crane (13)

Pizza And Chips

It's Friday night and I can bet
I know what I'm going to get
I can smell the aroma in the air
Of cheesy pizza, deep fried chips
And garlic bread for us to share.

Juicy tomatoes and melted cheese
My mum and dad aim to please
I can't begin to tell you how lovely it tastes
And I think you will agree
There's only one way to find out for yourself
And that's to taste it and see.

Kiam Read (11)

Spaghetti Bolognese

I sit at the table
Waiting patiently for my meal
Fork at the ready
Aroma so strong I can almost feel . . .

I can feel a rumble in my tummy
I know it's on its way
I know its going to taste yummy
It's going to make my day.

Mince, onions and garlic bread too
Peppers, courgette, mushrooms
If you want to.

Spaghetti, pesto and olive oil
Spaghetti Bolognese is the food above all.

Lucy Cyhanchuk (11)

Poem Of Colour

My favourite colour is red
I'm not so keen on pink
I don't like yellow and blue
Because I think they stink
Black and brown are grotty
White just makes me sick
If you think I like purple
You must be really thick
Grey is a miserable colour
Orange is nice and bright
And you can't disagree
Cos you know I'm right!

Kelly Wells (11)

Brussels And Candyfloss

Brussels, they're gross
They're round, fat and green
They taste like, well Brussels
And there is nothing more foul
And there's nothing more mean
Brussels are so rubbish, don't go eatin' 'em.

Candyfloss is pink and fluffy
It is so very lovely
You get it in so many colours
Pink, yellow, white and green
It is served on a wooden stick
So you'd better eat it very quick.

Alex Vann (12)

I Love Pie

I love pie
Because of the taste
It keeps me going through the winter's race
Eat it for
Dinner
Breakfast
Or lunch
Or even by yourself
At brunch
Don't be hasty
Pies are tasty
I love pie!

Rebecca Upsall (12)

A Baby's Life

There are so many people around looking at me
Why?
What do they want?
Where did they come from?
Who are they?
They came from nowhere and now they're here to stay.

I feel confused and scared
What is going on?
Why do I feel this way?
I wonder why, I wonder why?

I'm starting to feel OK
I can feel
I can see more
I understand
I now feel secure and happy.

I am smaller than them
Softer and smoother than them
They are crowding me
Feeling me
Holding me
I like it!

The more secure they make me the more I like it
Keeping me so warm
Touching my skin
And playing with my hands
It's nice!
I feel safe now I understand I am a life, a gift to Earth!

Leah MacFarlane (14)

Sweets

Guess what I am? A sweet
A mouth-watering sweet
Sometimes I am nice and sometimes I am foul
Being on the shop shelf, hoping someone will buy me
I am squashed in this bag, I am hot
At last I say, someone has come to eat me
I ran and I tried to hide at the bottom of the bag
Every time I am first out of the bag
So what's the bet, I am first again
Please do not eat me, I am not nice
What am I on about? I am the best, so don't eat me
Man! I wish I was a green sour one
Oh well, I am a lovely strawberry one
Everyone loves me. They always eat me first
Oh no, here comes the horrible hand of doom
It's coming to me
I may look nice but I am horrible inside
I'll hide behind this green sour one
That was close, he took him and spat him out
If I try and get to the top I might get out
But do I want to be free?

Harry Hummel (13)

Football

The ball goes backwards and forwards like a dog chasing a toy
People starting to run around after it
Sometimes people get scared of it
But other times people just run with it
And try and score goals for their team
They get hurt but they get up again
Nothing will keep them down
Some are tall, some are small
Some are good, some are poor
But as long as they try their best
They might get somewhere in life.

Paige Smith (14)

The Battered Dog

Today I stand here luckily with four legs
I also lay here on newspaper
For the comfort of my bed
With my family in the living room
Eating crunchy Doritos with chilli sauce
How do they treat me?
With no respect
I stand up eager for food
As one trots into the kitchen
With an empty place
The one fiercely turns around and kicks me
Only kicks me in the ribs
I whimper with sadness back in my bed
What a life I have
With a family like this
A little amount of food I eat every day
How I starve is like death threatening
No water to drink
Because of the heat of the house
I bark with starvation
The master of the house then gets up
He walks towards me with gritted fists
He grabs me by the collar and boots me outside
Meanwhile, he quickly slaps me around the head
I growl with pain
As the master enters back in
I find escape with another family
What a family, that causes so much pain!
A family from Hell!

Leah James (14)

Just Because!

Just because we go to the park
Just because we wear Nike and Ecko
Doesn't mean we go around drinking, smoking and smashing
We just sit, chat or play some football.

Someone rings up the police with a complaint
Down come the police, search us from time to time
While someone's lying in the road from a hit and run driver
Or someone is being robbed.

We're just having a kick around
The way people stop and stare
As if to say it was you
The way they sometimes speak to you.

Can't they just leave us alone
And not pick up the phone?
Just because we wear these clothes
Just because . . . just because . . .

Michael Webster (14)

Blind, Blind!

I'm blind
What is the problem?
All I want is a normal life
Even though I don't get one!

People stop and stare
I can just tell
I love attention
But not in that way.

My dog is my knight in shining armour
He loves me how I am
If he wasn't here right now
I couldn't survive.

My life with no eyes is dreadful
I'm only a kid
My name is Roxy
I'm glad I won't live!

Rebecca Wakeling (13)

My Brother

Bedford was the place we met
In a big play area
Although I didn't talk to him much
I looked at him through the nets.

I played with his son Shane
He is so sweet
But they call him a pain
As he's always under their feet.

He picked me up from school one day
So I rushed out to see him
We went to the shops to get some sweets
And he bought me loads of chocolate.

We wrote letters to each other
Talking about everything
Then one day he didn't write back
Then I found out why.

He got into trouble
And was sent to prison
Since then I've not spoken to him
One day I hope I will
Ben, my brother.

Samantha Stuart (13)

Bully

They trip me and I fall
I hear them call my name.
'What a geek,' I hear them call,
'Look at him, he's so lame.'

I hear them make sarcastic remarks
Some are worse than others,
'Where did he get his clothes, Clarks?'
They take the mick out of your sisters and brothers.

They use horrid words like fat, ugly and chink
There are quite a few
Do they not think?
There's a lot of them, enough for a queue.

I can't do anything
Apparently, nor can my school
They call people names like weird and puffin
My school does nothing but sits and drool.

Some spit, some punch
Some bully until they have your kit
Some do it at break, some do it at lunch.

I'll get revenge some day
It's these people I detest
On what those nasty bullies say
Oh why won't they give it a rest?

But I'm just the bullied
It doesn't matter what I say
No matter how much I beg and plead
They still get their own way.

I'm the bullied
They're the bullies.

Daniel Probert (13)

A Homeless Life

Where I am I cannot sit on a seat
Instead I lay there in the street
As the rain comes down like a river
It goes through my veins and makes me shiver.

Here I am, drowning in my sorrow
When will I be free? I don't know
Maybe today, maybe tomorrow
It seems like time is ticking . . . so slow.

I cannot help but weep
Every night when I go to sleep
A long time ago I had a wife
But then I lost her, along with my life.

A lot of people tend to stare
Sometimes I wonder if they care
They point and think it's funny
But it's hard without any money.

Ryan Humphreys (13)

Homeless!

I was born on the 4th November 1989
That's when I began to grow
I was 17, in a matter of time
So sad and low
I walked out one day
I've never been back there
Surviving without pay
No spare pennies for a fare
All I sleep on is a sack
People walking by with heads above
People putting posters up with tack
All I want is some love
What did I ever do so wrong?

Chloe Whittle (14)

I Wish I Was Normal

I'm in a wheelchair
And nearly lost my life
I was in a car crash
And I haven't lived the same life
I feel better in a wheelchair
Than being a person locked in unable to move
The way people stop and stare
Just because I can't move and groove
People can't help looking
But I wish they did. Stop glaring
Just because I'm different then
I'm not normal to them - ever.
I don't want to be a clone of someone
I want to be less unique
People don't even try to help
If they did I'd feel defeated
Anyway, I wish that I could walk and groove
I just want to be normal.

Michelle Small (14)

We Are Yobs!

Yobs, we are the ones that wear the hoodies
Lots of us hang around in the park
We are not the goodies, we are the baddies
We cause riots after dark.

Yobs, we are normally kids as you know
If we see the police, we run
We are the ones that have the ASBOs
We will beat you up just for fun.

Yobs, we put our hoods up so we don't get seen
We like to get drunk on the streets
We like to be really, really mean
When it's your birthday we will give you beats.

Yobs, we will rob your house and take all your money
We will smash the window or break down the door
We think this is very funny
We will do anything, even if we break the law.

Tom Rowe (13)

What Is It?

It's a cold wet night
Sitting on my step
'My step' meaning my home
With no food . . . not a bite
This is unfairness.

People just walk by
As if I'm just not there
I'm dying here, can't you see?
But I know that they don't care
This is ignorance.

Cardboard sheets are what I lie on
And a ledge that stands above
I wish I had somebody
Somebody that I could love
This is my life.

Rosie Kirk (14)

A Celebrity

I can't go anywhere without being noticed
Is it because I am famous?
I wish I was not noticed
Sometimes I just want to quit
It is good to have money
But sometimes I just don't care.

Everywhere are photographers
So I can't even go to the shops
I have to get someone to do it
So I do not get harassed.

When I have to go somewhere
I have to wear a hat
So I can live in the shadows
And that's the end of that.

Scott Eaton (14)

The Meaning Of Life?

There's no answer
Is there one?
No, not the cure for cancer
But this question I dwell upon
Maybe it's Heaven, maybe it's Hell
Is it your soul you are willing to sell?
To shout, to sing
Nobody knows
Deep inside the anticipation grows
To be happy, to be sad
Maybe it's about you being good or bad.
To feel wanted, to feel loved
To touch the sky high above
Experiences maybe
Shame people didn't see . . .
So, what is this question I hear you ask?
What is the meaning of life?

Nicole Manship (14)

Meaning Of Life

Ask yourself the meaning of life?
This is everybody's dream
Settle down, be happy and find a wife
We are all in this together, so let's be a team
Forget about the fights and the war
Let's all be happy
And open the happiness door
Not long till we die
So live it a bit more
Why are we here?
What is it for?

Tom Prickett (14)

Turning Back Time

Everyone makes mistakes
But we can't always put them right
You wish you could
But the clock's ticked a little too far
Do we mean to make them
Or is it a reaction from head to toe?
Why? On purpose?
Did you think it was cool and fun
By accident . . .
It's a regret not something to smile about
Turning back time
To meet famous people in history
This is a wish not a regret
This could be fun and seen as impossible
It's almost a dream
A dream incomplete
So why think of this?
It's beneath our feet
We live to dream
Dream to live
So why . . . ?
Why fantasise on turning back time?
It's never going to happen
It's not amazing
Just a mess up with time
So this is fake
So why think of it . . . ?

Jessica Dempsey (13)

Meaning Of Life

Why are we here?
To sit in the pub and drink beer?
There is a reason
For us being here
The buildings, the wildlife
The land and the water
Who made this place?
Are we here to do good or evil?
To climb a mountain
Or to swim with a seal?
We are here to fill
Our lives with ambitions.

Anthony Stott (14)

A Cat's Day

I lay here sleeping all day
In this lovely house
This is my spot where I lay
No noises, not even a mouse.

My favourite thing is catnip
My owner lets me play with it
Then after I will have another kip
Then I'll go for a wander, to stay fit.

I can do whatever I wish
And go wherever I want
In a pond I shall catch a fish
I hope it's as big as an elephant.

Now I am going to bed
And I will have a great dream
I must go now to rest my head
And dream of big fish in a stream.

Megan Heggs (12)

Turn Back Time

If I could turn back time
I would see my grandad again
To remember how he sounds
Take a trip down memory lane.

I would say how much I love him
And how I miss him so
How I will never forget him
How I wish he never had to go.

I would tell him my great achievements
That the future holds
I'd give him a great big kiss
And seal it in gold.

Seeing him would be great
But this is just a rhyme
If only it could be
And I could turn back time.

He'd hold me close and say
Like he always did
You're my little rascal
My gorgeous little kid.

I would talk to him for ages
But the time would fly
At least I had that moment
To say one last goodbye.

Heather Garrigan (13)

Life

The meaning of life is that we landed here on Earth
We are all celebrities watched by the real world
They have watched us forever
Ever since we landed on this so-called Earth
They have been gazing at us developing into humans
Laughing to themselves, we are used for entertainment.

Jason Green (14)

Fairy-Tale World . . .

I am a little princess
Whatever I want I get
Life is so perfect
My world is simply set.

My mummy loves me
So much I scream
My daddy loves me
So much he fulfils my dreams.

I live in a castle
With my horse named Tinkerbell
We have so much fun
I will love Tinkerbell forever, I shall, I shall!

I have found my prince
Who said, 'Death do us part.'
We had our little baby
Who completed my heart.

I am a little princess
Whatever I want I get
Life is just so perfect
My world is simply set.

Remi Smith (13)

A Mind Of A Baby

I feel as though there is something on me
I get lots of attention
People picking me up and cuddling me
I feel like I am in prison.

It's not fair
People look to see who I look like
I have no hair
So I look more like Uncle Mike.

I don't know what I am drinking
Or even what I eat
I could be drinking anything
It might be disgusting meat.

It's too hot
This is really steep
Why do I sleep in a cot?
I want to go to sleep.

Laura Pugh (13)

Meaning Of Life

To win money?
To play a game?
To be funny?
To get fame?
What is the meaning?

To eat and drink?
To hate all boys?
To love pink?
To play with toys?
What is the meaning?

To learn a tune?
Reach for a star?
To touch the moon?
Go to a bar?
What is the meaning?

To breathe fire?
Swim with a shark?
To have a desire?
Have a lark?

To love or hate?
Work it out yourself mate!

Beth Corby (11)

Football!

I am feeling really scared
As if all of England cared
As I step up to take the shot
It will feel like I have hit the jackpot.

As the crowds chant
Steve Gerrard, Gerrard
He passes from forty yards
He's big and his shots are hard
Steve Gerrard, Gerrard.

If I score this shot I'll have all the cash
If I miss this shot I'll be over in a flash
If we lose this game I'll be hated for years
If we win this game the fans will drink their beers.

Steve Gerrard, Gerrard
He passes from forty yards
He's big and his shots are hard
Steve Gerrard, Gerrard.

As I take my shot it hits the bar
But Rooney runs up and shoots and scores
As Rooney's shot was shot from far
And now I can go home and have my snores.

Kane Bradshaw (11)

Life

What is it?
Is it love?
Is it hate?
Is it something really great?

No one knows what it could be
Is it something you cannot see?
Take life on the chin
And don't just dream about being thin!

What is it?
Is it smooth?
Is it rough?
Is it something really tough?

No one knows what it could be
Just let it run swimmingly and free
Make sure you have a good chat
And don't worry if you're a little bit fat!

What is it?
Is it happy?
Is it sad?
Is it something really bad?

No one knows what it could be
Is it something between just you and me?
You have to believe in yourself
So don't just sit around, leap off your shelf!

Rosie-Ann Higgins (11)

The Alien

I am an alien
I'm stuck on Mars
When I look up
All I see are stars.

I really wish
I could go to Earth
Live on my own
Bit of turf.

But people might
Be scared of my looks
They are not like
What you see in books.

So please can you help me
Out of this place?
I need to pack
My empty case.

Jadine Walbrook (12)

A Baby's Poem

Why are they so tall
Standing way up high
Near where aeroplanes fly?
Why am I so small?
Oh yes, I'm only a baby after all.

Why have they got staring eyes
So bright and wide
Following me from side to side?
Why are mine as small as flies?
Oh yes, I'm only a baby after all.

Why have they got muscly legs
So big and strong
Stronger than King Kong?
Why are mine as skinny as pegs?
Oh yes, I'm only a baby after all.

Now I am so tall
Standing way up high
Near where aeroplanes fly
Now they are so very small
Oh yes, they're only babies after all.

Reece Johnson (13)

Football!

You have come so far
Don't mess it up
Tie your bootlace
Keep your head up.

It's time to kick off
The whistle blows
Everyone cheers
So keep on your toes.

He passes the ball
It's time to strut your stuff
Round four players, *bang!*
One goal just isn't enough!

Callum Bingham (13)

Lost In A Dream

L ifting a building from country to country
O pening up a chest of pure gold
S tealing every jewel in the universe
T oppling down a hill made of chocolate *dreams*

I n and out of dream to dream
N ever stopping, like endless rivers . . . *dreams*

A nd more to come . . . *dreams*

D eadly spiders scuttle over the water, following you everywhere
R unning from man-eating people
E ating along with Adam and Eve
A mazing creatures all coming out of a bag
M illions and millions of dreams to go . . . *dreams.*

Jake Brimley (13)

Food Around The World

The French have snails with their Sunday lunch
The gooey centre is the best in the west
The French have frogs' legs, *munch, munch, munch*
This is one of your 5-a-day, mmmm, they're the best.

Mexicans breathe fire all the time when they eat their spice
The deadly hot sauce eats at your tongue
Now listen tight, cold melted cheese will freeze you like ice
Now when you journey across a hot plate it will always burn your lungs.

Now here's my favourite
Pizza and ice cream
The Italians know how to serve
It's the very best in the whole wide world.

Ryan Green (12)

Monster

There was a monster long ago
From an island off the shore of Cornwall
It caused lots of terror
And killed lots of people
And sent them all to Heaven.

Along came our man
Who had a plan
To catch this evil thing
As strong as a bull and
As sly as a fox he found this monster thing.

He ran away to avoid being slain
But the hero just caught him up
He hid behind a mound
And sprang out of the ground
And cornered the hero.

They had a fight and the monster got a fright
As he got killed as well.

Harry Demetriou (11)

War Boat

Always waiting for someone to untie me
Put yourself in my shoes and you will see
How unloved I am to the men
Left on my own like a sheep in a pen
Waiting, waiting.

I have very tatty sails
And worn out rusty nails
Neglected and old
And starting to grow mould
Rotting, rotting.

Lonely and wet
Only I can bet
They won't come back and untie me
An abandoned city is what I see
Watching, watching.

I can see a person, I think it's a man
I watched and watched, he ran and ran
He came to untie me, I know I would last
I don't care anymore, it's all in the past
Happy, happy.

Katie Walker (12)

What Is The Meaning Of Life?

What has the world come to?
What have we become?
Why are we fighting each other?
Can we undo what we have done?

What is the meaning of life?
Is it to care for the sick and disabled?
Do we have to stop world poverty
Or respect people more able?

Do we have to be a celebrity
Or meet the Queen?
Do we have to get a knighthood
Or fulfil a lifelong dream?

Why isn't everyone nice?
Why can't we be at peace?
That is just a factor of life
Don't worry, just live with ease.

Alex O'Connell (12)

My Life Is Hard

I am poor
Can you open a door?
I live in a box
But no one knocks.

People say I'm nothing
But I can be loving
I need a home
Or just a loan.

My box is damp
I'm more of a tramp
So take me away
To somewhere I can stay.

I have no money
But I eat raw honey
And send me a card
Because my life is hard.

Liam Davy (11)

The Pitch

The game has started
The whistle is blown
The players have parted
Get on the phone.

A corner is given
But not to us
The football is driven
Without a fuss.

The ball is now
At the back of my mouth
The opposition has scored
A good shot from the south.

The crowd is roaring
Jumping out of their seats
The linesmen are snoring
Just in time with the beat.

Megan Footman (11)

A Lonely Tramp

Every day is long and lonely
Every day feels like prison
Every day just passes by.

I look around and see happy people
In winters I sit there freezing cold
In summers I sit there scorching hot
For I am a lonely tramp
No one cares about me.

Rich and happy people walk by leaving me nothing
I am so hungry
And all I want is a little comfort but just get ignored
I want to be loved but I am hated.

I am so hungry
All I own is ragged clothes and a blanket
I see shops with lots of nice warm clothes
I smell food in the air.

Declan Lonergan (13)

She Wasn't Ready For This Baby

Today a girl is born
A girl called Stacey
A girl without a dad
Her mother was raped
She wasn't ready for this baby.

Her mother was a prostitute
Sold herself for money
But after everything she went through
She wasn't ready for this baby.

Social Services crowded around
And threatened to take Stacey
But she stood her ground
And told them they wouldn't take Stacey
Even though she wasn't ready for this baby.

Stacey's grown up, now 18 years old with a husband
Her mother is now a social worker
Stacey got to see her mum
And her mum turned to her and said,
'You've turned into a beautiful young lady.'
Stacey started to cry,
'Mother I have something to tell you
I've turned out like you, I lied
I'm not ready for this baby.'

Sarah-Jane Hammonds (14)

The Sandy Beach

Walking across the beach in my bare feet
The sand goes all in-between my toes
The sand burns all in-between my toes
The sand is like flashing gold all around
The seashore
The sun starts to go down
The moon shoots up and shines on the sea
The sea is covered in little stars flashing away
So the sea is shiny
I walk into the warm sea
I just feel like going to sleep in the sea
I wake up in the morning
And see the sun shining
I'll just walk again down the beach
And try and make it like last week.

Alex Busby (14)

Global Warming

Global warming, Oh I hate it so much
Global warming filling our world
Global warming raising our seas
Global warming melting our ice.

Global warming and the greenhouse effect
Destroying our homes, killing our food.

Global warming I wish it would stop
Global warming damaging our future, destroying our past
Oh I wish global warming would stop.

Global warming, what can it do?
Global warming destroying homes
Global warming killing our laughter.

Global warming killing our fish
Global warming killing our trees
Global warming killing our children.

Global warming what can I do?
Global warming
What can you do?

Adam Kindleyside (13)

Best Friends Forever

We were best friends Abigail and me
Then we parted, setting us both free
People see me sad
But they don't know the fun times I've had
They see me depressed and do not ask why
Even when they see me cry.

These new schools have set us far apart
But we will remember each other still at heart.

These eight years have gone so quick
But I wish they had gone slower.

We're still best friends
We met in the swimming pool
But now we are separated by these new schools.

I hope I will see her again
Then we can be friends together
For ever and ever, still best friends.

Jake Moore (14)

Just Words

Why am I here?
Do I have a purpose?
Why can't I speak?
I want to shout out to everyone
Tell them I'm lonely
They don't listen
I'm confused
Why are all these people here?
Where am I?
What am I doing here?
I'm hungry and tired
I had dreams of this place
It was happy and quiet
Oh so quiet!

Lauren Shepherd (14)

A Blushing Bride

My legs are like jelly
I'm a blushing bride
I've butterflies in my belly
Where is all the pride?

My gorgeous groom is waiting
It's the best day of my life
So why am I hesitating?
I want to become his wife.

I'm walking towards the altar
To my gorgeous groom
I hope I do not falter
There's silence in the room.

My gorgeous groom has said, 'I do'
Oh now I feel the pride
I've spoken those words too,
'You may kiss the blushing bride.'

Bryony Garrigan (13)

Homeless Thoughts

As I lay under the cardboard fast asleep
People who walk by start to peep
I lay silent all day and all night cold
I think I'm ill because I've gone bald.
I see people staring and laughing at me
All I want is a nice cup of tea
At night when it's dark I start to cry
Because of cuts and bruises and things in my eye.
I lay at night looking at the stars
Shivering and crying whilst hearing the cars
All I want is a nice comfy bed
Instead of sleeping outside or in a garden shed.
I look through the bins for something to eat
Whilst limping around because of my mouldy feet
I sometimes sit around and start to pray
Wishing for somewhere warm and nice to stay.
But all of those wishes will never come true
Because I have no money and no help from you
And if you don't know what it's like on the street
I'm always in pain with a tiny heartbeat.

Christopher Weston (13)

Death

No summer, no winter, no morning or night
I only see demons and darkness, no light
Voices of children and elderly cries
I have to stop it by taking their lives.

My job is a dark one, full of despair
But as much as I want to, I simply don't care
I do not hear voices or think in my head
And I only see humans once they are dead.

I feel your pain and agony too
I would give anything just to be you
No family, no parents or sister or brother
But off I must go to slaughter another.

I'm sorry you're dead child, but it was your time
I feel as if I have committed a crime
Killing and killing, all I do is watch and sit
My name is Death, child, live with it.

Jacob Smith (12)

My Baby Sister

Everyone is bigger than me
They all pick me up
Kissing me and hugging me
It all gets too much.

I love my mummy, daddy and sister too
But most of all I love Winnie the Pooh
I can't live without my white chocolate
My mum says my sister sounds like Catherine Tate.

I love getting messy
I don't clean it up
That's what my mum does
She cleans me up.

I don't have to do anything
I love being young
Watching Mum do everything
Oh yes, this is love!

Lola Witherington (13)

Chihuahua

Look, I'm a Chihuahua
I'm not a scrawny rat
And the thing that annoys me most
Is when you mistake me for a cat.

You can put me in your handbag
You can dress me up in clothes
You can take me to the salon
And in return I'll lick your nose!

Just because I'm a Chihuahua
Doesn't mean big dogs can get me
I may fool you with little legs
But I can run extremely quickly.

Someone hurry up and buy me
I really hate being alone
I don't need very much
Someone please take me home!

Shannen Clark (12)

Ouch! That Hurts!

Ouch! That hurts!
My owner keeps on my back
My back is really aching now
I wish I could go in the bath
That will help me to relax
No, stop, that hurts! *Ow, ow ow!*
I'm supposed to be a loveable thing
That is how I'm designed
But I wish I had wings
That will be fine.

Everyone touches me
Feels me and worst of all bends me
Why can't they leave me alone
I wish I was hard to see
But it's like a dog to a bone.

I am a bendy ruler
Which I don't really want to be
My owner makes me smoother
By touching and bending me.

Mark Jones (12)

But I Could Only Wish . . .

All these people talking
I don't hear a word
I see their lips moving
But everything is silent.

I try to speak
But I don't know how to
Everything is making a sound
But it's only me who cannot hear.

I feel so alone
I could only imagine
What it would be like
But I can only see.

The wind blowing
The trees rustling
The lapping of the ocean
I would give anything

But I can only wish . . .

Samantha Higgs (12)

Unwanted?

I am forever sitting here
On this shelf full of toys
I try never to shed a tear
I am just a doll, an unwanted doll.

I am picked up and stared at
Through round, placid eyes
But I'm put back where I was sat
I am just a doll, an unwanted doll.

All the other toys are quickly sold
But I am left collecting dust
Why am I never picked - am I too old?
I am just a doll, an unwanted doll.

All the new dolls I envy so much
Their clothes are so much nicer
However, they aren't so different as such
I am just a doll, an unwanted doll.

I am picked up once more
And stared at through affectionate eyes
Over to the counter I am carried - I'm sure
I am a doll, a wanted doll!

In two warm arms I am cuddled
I have never felt so happy
On a shelf I shall no longer be huddled
I am a doll, a loved doll!

Jessica Russell (13)

Growing Up!

I was in the most beautiful place
But now I've been pushed from my special space
And so I've joined the human race
I'm just a baby, a little baby.

All I know, I'm in a world that's round
And here I am hearing a new sound
The place I lay is like a dog pound
I'm just a baby, a little baby.

Then I see something big, something . . . like my mum
I know, I'm sure as I'm not dumb
From now on she'll be my best chum
I'm just a baby, a little baby.

Soon I find out something new
It's been sometime now and now I'm two
My favourite toy pet is called Blue
Now I'm a kid, just a little kid.

Owen Williams (13)

The Projector

I am a projector
I am made by someone called Epson
They only gave me one eye
Sometimes I want to die.

On and off all day long
Bored of doing what other people want me to do
I will not last forever, I will break soon
The nights are dark and I just want to turn on.

Hundreds of people forget I am here
I put my effort in, where's my merit?
I am never cleaned, cared for or respected
But I am here for everyone else to enjoy.

I am bored of being a projector
Why can't I change?
A table I have always wanted to be
Why me?

Adam Harlow (13)

Why Are We Here?

Why are we here?
What are we for?
We must have a purpose
But how to be sure?

Why are we here?
What do we have to do?
We must have a purpose
But lost many centuries ago.

Why are we here
In a world so cruel?
We must have a purpose
Or are we just fools?

Why are we here?
Where are we meant to be?
We must have a purpose
It's not easy to see.

Jamie Mullineaux (13)

Living In The Cinders

My life is such a shame
Living in the cellar
Cinderella is my name
It's hard to even tell ya!

I am so very jealous
Working in the dirt
Of my wealthy sisters
This feeling starts to hurt.

My name is rather annoying
As that is all I hear
It is eventually destroying
My confidence with my peers!

Waiting for Prince Charming
It has taken years and years
It sounds rather alarming
That I've not shed any tears.

One day I hear a noise
A sound I will always remember
A cheer outside my window
Even in late December!

I rush to the door
Out into the freezing snow
There I stand in awe
As the prince bows down very low!

He says loud and clear,
'Marry me Cinderella!'
I shout, 'Why, of course my dear
And I'm never going back to the cellar!'

Katherine Ardley (13)

Crunch!

When I get chewed, I make a bone-crunching sound
The thing I hate most is being thrown to the ground
When I hit the floor I make a leap and a bound
As I lay there on the ground, people look in disgust at what
they've found.

The best moment is being the chosen one
Put in a packet and then I am gone
Out again to be in and shown
Eaten up all on my own.

This is worth it, I need not fight
Up and down and taking flight
I am always at parties during the night
Popped out and in and there goes the light.

This is the end, the story of me
My first and last name is Toffee
In the mouth I go splat
This is the end and that is that!

Max Anderson (13)

If I Was In America . . .

If I was in America
I would be the happiest boy in the world.
If I was in America
I would go to Disney World and meet all the characters
Who starred in books and films for generations.
If I was in America
I would go to the best golf courses that America has to offer
Where legendary golfers have played
If I was in America
I would go to the Grand Canyon, one of the natural wonders of the
world
If I was in America
I would go to Hollywood to see the streets which are paved with gold.
If I was in America
I would go to Graceland, the home of 'The King'
If I was in America
I would go to New York to see the Empire State Building
One of the tallest buildings in the world
If I was in America
I would travel along Route 66
If I was in America
I would go to the White House where the President lives
If I was in America . . .

Ben Cluskey (12)

My Cat Sally

My cat Sally is as silly as a clown
Her colours are white and gingery brown
She plays and fights with other cats
And loves to kill dirty old rats
She sits and watches the birds pass by
And stares and begins to whine and cry
She loves to sleep in my nana's armchair
The only trouble is she covers it with hair
She sleeps for most of the day
The only time she isn't is when she wants to come and play
So my cat Sally is as silly as a clown.

Emma Tones (13)

Food

I love cheese
Cheese is the best
It looks disgusting when it's blue
It also smells like it too.

I love cookies they are soft and sweet
I wonder what tastes my tongue will meet
When I buy one I'm in for a treat
I don't really like the ones made from wheat.

Chocolate, chocolate is so great
But please don't eat it after eight
If you eat it that late
You will never be my mate.

Food is good all in all
Some foods are big and some foods are small
You can buy most foods from the shopping mall
When you have bought them this is best of all
You can eat them in a dining hall.

Zara Cook (12)

Love And Hate

Love is a kiss down in the park
Love is hearing a baby dog bark
Love is seeing a smile when right
Love is Ant and Dec on a Saturday night
Love is . . .

Hate is as bad as an evil look
Hate is writing a nasty book
Hate looks like an evil crook
Hate is looking at a piece of muck
Hate is . . .

Love is an angel up in the sky
Love guides you through this evil life
Love is a special candlelit night
Love is someone that kisses you right
Love is . . .

Hate is a scary vicious face
Hate is a chilly cold fireplace
Hate is like a freezing house
Hate is squealing at a dead mouse
Hate is . . .

Abi Goyns (13)

Colour Poem

Red is fire that burns so bright
Yellow is the stars that twinkle at night
Orange is the fruit that tastes so sweet
Pink is the colour of a baby's feet
Purple is lavender so soothing and calm
Blue is the tractor on the farm
Indigo is the sky between day and night
Green is the luscious green grass in the spring so light
Turquoise is the calming Caribbean sea
Lilac is the bush which is loved by the bee
Cerise is the colour of a little girl's dress
Black is the colour you can wear to impress
Brown is the mud where flowers grow
White is the snowballs that we throw.

Robyn Braker (12)

Young Writers Information

We hope you have enjoyed reading this book - and that you will continue to enjoy it in the coming years.

If you like reading and writing poetry drop us a line, or give us a call, and we'll send you a free information pack.

Alternatively if you would like to order further copies of this book or any of our other titles, then please give us a call or log onto our website at www.youngwriters.co.uk

**Young Writers Information
Remus House
Coltsfoot Drive
Peterborough
PE2 9JX**

(01733) 890066